A Book of Simple Rituals

Wendy Wilson

Contents

Rituals Included in this Book

A Book of Easy Rituals
Introduction

This is a book of easily-staged. ready-to-use rituals to celebrate the eight Wiccan holidays. Of all the rituals I have written, led and published over the years, I have chosen 10 of the easiest for this book. There is one for each of the Wiccan holidays, plus a healing ritual and a ritual of self-improvement.

The rituals included in this book are oriented to small gatherings of, perhaps six to 13 people. The rituals are scaled to fit in a living room or a small backyard. Some rituals may be scaled up for larger groups. Some of them can be scaled down to accommodate just a couple of people.

This is a part of my personal "Book of Shadows," which is a record of many of the rituals that I have written over the last 20 years. I have included some rituals that conveyed their central themes clearly and were easy to put together in a practical, logistic sense. Each ritual is based on a central theme derived from Neo-Pagan and Wiccan traditions. I pull one idea or tradition and build a ritual that involves the participants in that idea. I have also used current scientific theories, natural phenomena and spiritual ideas, both my own and those of others around me.

The rituals are also reflections of my ideas of deity and reality, which may or may not be the generally held ideas. A long time ago, as a new Wiccan, I read the works of Marion Weinstein and Scott Cunningham. The concept that "the witch is the magic" resonated with me and has permeated my rituals, spells and way of thinking. I believe that each of us is the magical child, born of the earth and, as Carl Sagan said, made of "star stuff." I believe that we only need to look within ourselves for deity. This is certainly not a new thought, but it is a good and powerful one.

Furthermore, I take seriously the idea that Wicca is a religion of experience. Ritual is a right brain activity – words only carry the message, they do not convey the truth. No book, no lecture, no sermon can bring us an understanding of a larger reality. Ritual can do this because it takes us from the place of work and home and family to a separate place, a place outside of everyday concerns and worries. Within that separate place, ritual can bring the participant to a mind state where the perception of the extra-ordinary is possible. This may not always happen, and it may not happen often, but it is possible.

As I became more involved and dedicated to my practice of Wicca, I began to develop ideas on how a ritual should be constructed. I have certain goals in mind for my rituals. I prefer rituals where everyone participates – we all get to be a part of the ceremony – because action is more interesting for the participants. It gets the point of the ritual across better than people just standing around talking, or worse, a priest or priestess just standing around talking. I try to structure some of the rituals so that, on occasion, the participant ends up with an object that can be taken home as a reminder of their work. Participants don't always leave with an object, of course, but on occasion they do.

Before we get started, here's a little more information about my rituals. They are short, so for most of them, everyone stands around the altar. Some traditions include a time for personal sharing before the main activity of the ritual. We usually do not include this, but these rituals are short enough that you could add some time for that. Traditionally, most Wiccan rituals include what is called "the simple feast" toward the end of ritual – a sharing of bread and wine or "cakes and ale". I sometimes feel that the ritual has ended logically at the end of the principal activity, so I don't always include a feast. Often the main activity carries us emotionally to the end of the ritual and adding anything would cause an abrupt and jarring transition. I want to keep the feeling of drama generated by the main ceremony as I end the ritual and open the circle. If you feel that not having the simple feast leaves out an important part of the ritual, feel free to include that as well.

These particular rituals were chosen because they call for a minimum of ritual tools or "props". Some of them have a few, simply made items, but they should be within the skill level of most. The exception is Beltane, but creation of a mini Maypole should be doable for most people.

Overall, the rituals that I have developed include a lot of candles and fire. I make a point of mentioning safety in my fire rituals, but I'd like to emphasize it here. Please be careful. A fire extinguisher is not out of place at a ritual. Tie your hair back and kilt up your skirts if you will be near fire. Flowing sleeves and skirts are traditional and romantic, but dangerous.

Some other things that I have found useful include sending a copy of the ritual out to each participant a week or so in advance of the ritual. This gives people a chance to see what will be done, how long it will take and what is expected of them. If you are including music, it's really essential for the participants receive the music ahead of time so that they can review it and be ready for the service. With or without music, sending the participants your ritual allows them to select roles, review their speaking parts and give you, the priestess or priest, useful ideas on the ritual's feasibility.

You will notice that, for the most part, the sheet music for the songs used in the ritual is not shown. Most of them are copyrighted, so you will have to Google them and download the music.

A couple of notes about the formatting in this book: I have italicized the text that is not intended to be spoken, so it is clear what is commentary, activity or "stage direction" and what is to be said aloud. Also, you will notice that the rituals are led by someone labeled priestess. The person running the event could be a priestess, priest or perhaps anyone who is comfortable taking on the responsibility to lead the ritual.

Lastly, I have relied on the traditions of Neo-Paganism and Wicca for ideas and for central themes. In many cases, I have also relied on the ideas of others as a starting place.

Occasionally, I have borrowed text from others, always with gratitude. Sometimes someone else has said it so well, that I didn't feel I could improve on it. Whenever I have borrowed an idea or some text, I have noted what I borrowed and from whom, and when possible, I have asked for permission. I think we need to have respect for one another's' work. So, I ask the same of you if you borrow some of my words or rituals. Please feel free to use these rituals and change them in any way, but please credit me if you use the text, and I ask that you do not re-publish this material for profit.

As we often say: Merry Meet!

Setting up for A Ritual

Now, some practical tips on setting up any ritual:
For every ritual, you will need a space for the ritual. For 6 or 8 people, a normal living room is usually sufficient. You may need to push the furniture back against the walls. In good weather consider holding the ritual outside if you have the space.

You will need a table for an altar along with the following items:
Four candles: one each of Yellow, red, blue, and green;
One or two white candles or one black and one white;
A compass;
A candle-snuffer;
Matches and an ashtray;
A bell or chime;
Your athame (ritual knife) or broom or wand;
Printed ritual programs, one for each participant.
Sheet music for any songs being sung
Each ritual will also include items specific to that ritual, which are outlined in the next section.

To set up the altar, place the colored candles in the holders. These are the directional candles. Using the compass to determine the compass points, place the yellow candle on the east side of altar. Place the red candle on the south side. Place the blue candle on the west side and the green candle on the north side. Position the white candles in the center of the altar. For some rituals, you may want to place the directional candles on the perimeter of the ritual circle, for safety or convenience. I have standing candle stands that I place at the cardinal points of the circle.

The other items should be put on the altar. If you are using a broom, you can lean it against the table. Some people also like to have incense on the altar. If any of the participants have asthma or other lung problems, you might want to smudge the room before the ritual and have nothing burning during the ritual. If your ritual includes a "simple feast" you will want to have cider or wine and cookies or bread as well. If it is just water, you need a pitcher of water and glasses. Often an altar cloth is used. If the altar is getting crowded, consider having a smaller table for things like the simple feast that will be used later in the rituals.

Items needed for each specific ritual are explained in the section on that ritual.

Every ritual also has "roles" for the participants. For every ritual, four people are needed to light the directional candles described above. This is called "calling the corners" or "the watchtowers." Before the ritual, decide who will be "east", who will be "south" and so on. Many rituals call for a "maiden" who is the helper for the priestess. Maidens can be any age or gender, but you might want to change the title to acolyte if the person volunteering as maiden is a middle-aged man or if you just want to use a non-gendered title.

Other roles specific to each ritual are discussed in the chapter for that ritual.

When you are setting up for a ritual it's a good idea to read through ritual and make a checklist of everything you are going to need. Include the programs and the music for any songs you are going to sing in the checklist. Send as much as you can out to the participants ahead of time. The music is particularly important.

Samhain

The Circle Never Ends

The Circle Never Ends
Setting up for This Ritual

This is a traditional Samhain ritual. It honors the other side of life and reminds us that death is a part of life. It could be used as a memorial service as well.

Setup

You need many candles. Samhain is a fire festival and I tried to honor that. There is a black and a white candle on the altar. A white candle represents incoming energy and the black candle represents departing energy.

Each participant will need a floating candle. Check one before the ritual to be sure it does not take on water and go out. You also need a taper to light the floating candles. Use an altar cloth that you don't mind getting candle wax on, since you assuredly will. And of course, there are the four directional candles.

You will need a shallow bowl or platter of water to float the candles on. You will need about 5 minutes of music for the meditation.

You need the fruit for the second part of the ritual. Before the ritual, ask each person to go to the market and select an apple to bring with them. They will place these on the altar at the start of the ritual. You will need also need one pomegranate and you should probably have a few apples on hand for participants who forget to bring one. You will need a knife to cut the apples with. If your athame is not sharp enough, bring a knife from the kitchen. Dull knifes are dangerous. Bring a small cutting board, too. Cutting an apple in one's hand is dangerous. When you cut the apple, cut it crosswise, across the "equator", not from the top to the bottom.

So, you will need:
One white candle
One black candle
One taper to light the floating candles
Floating candles, enough for all the participants
Bowl of water, large enough for all the candles
Matches or lighter
Short recorded musical piece for meditation.
One pomegranate
Apples, one per person
A Knife or athame
A Cutting board

The music for Round and Round We Go is available on the Web. Google the whole phrase: "Round and round we go, We hold each other's hands", otherwise you get a different song.

The Circle Never Ends
Order of Ritual

Clearing the Circle
The Priestess walks the perimeter of the circle.
Priestess: I clear this space of all negativity and bad feelings. I bless this time and this space for a ritual of spirit. Let no anger, hate or jealousy enter here. Here let only friendship be, in perfect love and perfect trust.

Calling the Quarters
Participant: I call the spirits of the east, whose voices open our minds to hear the past and the future.
Candle of the East is lit.
All: Blessed Be!

Participant: I call the spirits of the south, whose strength connect us to the spirits of others.
Candle of the South is lit.
All: Blessed Be!

Participant: I call the spirits of the west, whose emotions open our hearts to those who have journeyed west.
Candle of the West is lit.
All: Blessed Be!

Participant: I call the spirits of the north, the end of all journeys, that peace may hold us in her hands at the end of our travels.
Candle of the North is lit.
All: Blessed Be!

Raising the Temple
Priestess:
We set this time and place aside for ritual.

In this place that is no place and that is all places; In this time that is no time and that is all time, We stand between the worlds.
Ring bell.

Priestess: The temple is erected, let all who are here, be here in peace and love.

An Introduction to the Ritual
Priestess: This is Samhain, the Wiccan New Year's Eve, the Mexican Day of the Dead, the Catholic Day of Saints. We will celebrate the circle of life and death tonight.

All: There Is No End To The Circle.

The maiden lights the white and then the black candle.
Priestess: This is the twilight of the year, when the wheel turns to the quiet time of the year. The rich colors of flowers and foliage fade. As the green of summer fade away, our thoughts turn to those who have walked the circle of life before us.

In the fading of the year, the worlds of here and there, of material reality and of ethereal reality, of the manifest and the potential, feel mingled - not combined, not separate. Wisps of dreams, of feelings, of thoughts mix with the everyday. We feel the call of our own mortality. We hear the voices of those who sailed west before us. That part of them we carry in our hearts speaks clearly to us if we can listen.
During this evening, we will pause and gaze west, into the twilight, as the summer sets. We pause to hear those who would call our hearts. We remember with respect and love those now sleeping with Gaia.

Song
Sing:
Round and round we go, we hold each other's hands
and weave our lives in a circle, our love is strong, the dance goes on

Remembrance of Those Who Have Sailed West

We all turn and face West.
(Play music.)
We meditate, listening to the music, and then turn back to the altar.

Priestess: We light a candle to represent the love between our hearts and theirs.
Each person holds an unlit candle. Pause for thought.
Maiden pours water into cauldron. If she wishes, she says the name or names of those she is remembering.
Maiden floats her candle, then lights a taper from black candle and lights his/her candle and passes taper to next person. The next person does the same, mentioning the names of those being remembered or not, as he or she wishes. The priestess floats her candle last.

All:
We all come from the Goddess
And to her we shall return
Like a drop of rain,
Flowing to the ocean*

The Fruit of Life and the Fruit of Death

Priestess: We pause to remember that our stay here is brief. Each plant in its own time comes to the harvest, as will we. But our lives give rise to those who come after us. The pomegranate is a symbol of fertility and life, rounded and full of seeds, but when Persephone ate the seeds of the pomegranate, she was forced to stay in the underworld, the world of the dead, for 6 months. But she returned, because there is no end to the circle.
The Priestess goes to the altar and hold up the pomegranate. She says:
    Behold the Pomegranate, Fruit of Life ...
The athame is plunged into the pomegranate, splitting it open to display the seeds. She says:
    Whose seeds lie in the dormancy of death
The Priestess eats one of the seeds, saying:
    Taste the seeds of Death.

The pomegranate is then passed hand to hand through the participants of the ritual, each eating a seed and saying to the next person, saying: Taste the seeds of Death.

When it has come around:
Priestess: All life contains the seeds of death.
All: There is no end to the circle.

Priest or Priestess: The apple is the fruit of myth, too, the fruit of knowledge, the fruit that grows on the Isle of Avalon, the Summerland of the Wiccans.

The Priest or Priestess then holds up the apple, saying:
       Behold the apple: fruit of wisdom, fruit of death.
The apple is cut crosswise, saying:
       Which contains the symbol of life and self.
The apple is displayed, showing the inner pentagram,
Behold the five-fold star -- the elements of life: mind, body, emotion, wisdom, spirit.

The knife is passed from hand to hand. Each person then cuts their apple, saying: There is no end to the circle *and meditating on the circle of life, eats the apple.*

The Priest or Priestess: Death carries the seeds of life to the next generation.
All: There is no end to the circle.

Raising the Power
Priestess: We will now raise the power, feeling, as we raise it the power of those who have gone before and those who will come next.

Take the hand of the person on the right, saying, Hand-to-hand, we raise the power.

We raise the Power and then ground it.
Priestess: Now, touch the altar, feeling as you do, the power flowing from us, into the altar and down through the floor and spreading

through the earth, healing and strengthening the earth and supporting those who will live here after us.

Ending Reflection
Priestess: The northern hemisphere turns with the southern hemisphere, the moon reflects the sun, the palm moves with the hand. These things are not the same, yet they are each part of a whole. Life and death are the two halves of a whole -- without one, there cannot be the other.

The earth spins and the wheel turns to another year -- there is no end to the circle. In the year to come, let us face the winds and feel the rain, let us raise our faces to the sun. Let us live the year in peace and happiness.

Thanking the Quarters
Participant: Spirits of the East, Spirits of Air, we thank you for the winds that circle the earth.
Participant extinguishes the candle of East.
All: Blessed Be.

Spirits of the South, Spirits of Fire, we thank you for the fires of life that burn within.
Participant extinguishes the candle of South.
All: Blessed Be.

Spirits of the West, Spirits of Water, we thank you for the oceans that flow around the world.
Participant extinguishes the candle of West.
All: Blessed Be.

Spirits of the North, Spirits of Wisdom, we thank you for the rotating earth that brings us the seasons of life.
Participant extinguishes the candle of North.
All: Blessed Be.
Ring Bell

Opening the Circle

All: The circle is open but unbroken.
May the peace of the Goddess go in our hearts.
Merry meet, merry part, and merry meet again.
Blessed be.

*This was written by Z Budapest who allowed me to use it, if I recommend her website: http://www.zbudapest.com/ which I do with great pleasure and a bow to one of our community's elders.

Yule

Light Bringers

Light Bringers
Setting up for This Ritual

This ritual honors the miracle of the solstice. In it, we symbolically bring back the sun, by simulating the change in the day length leading up the solstice and then it's lengthening afterwards. We celebrate the change and look forward to the longer days.

Setup
There are some ritual tools or props for this ritual, but nothing too exotic or unobtainable.

The altar should have an incense burner with incense that has been lit, along with a large gold candle, which should be unlit.

Buy and light one gold candle before you buy all of them. Some folks found the scent objectionable or allergy-producing. If you think this is going to be a problem, substitute white or yellow candles for the altar and the participants.

The directional candles should be on stands at the perimeter of the circle, unlit. The Yule Log should also be on the altar as well as a bell. For the Yule Log, select a well-seasoned log about 24 inches long. Decorate it with paper ribbons and leaves. If you do not have a fireplace, substitute a yule log that is drilled for candles, and put candles in the holes.

If you are using the fireplace, A fire should be set and ready to light in it.

In addition, you will need smaller gold (or white) candles with candle-holders for each person and some long matches. Make sure that you have a candle snuffer on the altar. So here is the list:

Incense burner with incense (to be lit at beginning of ritual);
Large gold or white candle for the altar;

Small white candles, enough for each person (perhaps tea lights);
Long matches for the second part of the ritual;
Candle holders for the small candles (small dishes for tea lights);
Yule log (with candles if you do not have a fireplace);
Matches;
An ashtray;
A candle snuffer;
Percussion instruments.

The ritual begins with the participants outside the circle and they enter, one-by-one, to be greeted by the priestess at the eastern edge of the circle. So, the small candles placed in holders or on dishes should be on a table near where the participants will be entering the circle, so the priestess can hand them out.

At the beginning of the ritual, the long matches and an ashtray should be on the altar. If you are using tealights, the candles can be on saucers or small dishes. Matches and an ashtray should also be on the small table. There should be cake and cider along with glasses for each person, and a separate Yule blessing cup. If the altar is getting crowded, the cake and cider and the Yule blessing cup could be on a separate small table within the area that will become the circle.

Ask people to bring drums or other percussion instruments. The drums and instruments should be placed around the altar, on the floor if they are large. Have a couple of spare instruments on hand for the folks who forget.

Before the ritual starts, decide who will be participant one, and who will be participant two, and so on. Give the participants the verses assigned to that particular role. Each person should have their lines, either on separate sheets of paper or on programs with their portions highlighted. I usually send the participants' lines out to them ahead of time so that they can be become familiar with them.

In addition to the seven participants who will be reading the verses, there are some optional roles for a Yule Elder, a Holly King and an Oak King — if there are enough participants. If there are not enough, each person reads more than one verse and you can double up on the roles.

You will notice that the "quarters" are not called until late in the ritual, which is not the usual way, but the first part of the ritual is about calling the light and erecting the temple, so the calling of the quarters happens after that.

This is an **important** note: it is vital that the room be **totally dark** at the point when the first part of the second set of verses is said. This means that participant one should memorize the first verse of the second set, so it can be said in the dark. This is the verse just below the heading "The Coming of The Light" (see below.) For the other verses, readers may find a penlight helpful since it will still be somewhat dark.

I must credit my dearest friend with the verses in this ritual. They fit well and create the perfect rhythm. I am very grateful to him.

Light Bringers
Order of Ritual

Casting the Circle

The Circle is swept with a broom to sweep away the old darkness and make way for the new sun. The circle is cast. An implied door is created in the east using the motions of cutting a door. Here is where the participants will enter. The priestess stands at that opening, holding a lit candle.

Processional

As each participant enters the circle, the priestess hands the participant one of smaller candles. The participant lights his or her candle from the priestess's candle. The participant proceeds to the altar and puts the candle in one of the candleholders. If these are tea lights, then put them on saucers at the lighting. The participant then goes to the spot where he or she has put the instrument and begins drumming on a small drum or playing their percussive instrument.

Once the first participant has completed his or her actions, the second participant is greeted by the priestess and given a candle. The second proceeds to the altar to put his or her candle in a holder and takes a place in the circle, playing an instrument. This process continues until all the participants are at the altar. The Priestess closes the circle and proceeds to the altar to light a candle.

Drumming continues.
When the room is full of power, the Priestess makes sure all the electric lights are out and then signals to wind the drumming down. Drumming stops.

Priestess: We stand now at the threshold of the circle of time. Tonight, we celebrate Yule and the rebirth of the sun. Be here in perfect love and perfect trust.

An Introduction to the Ritual

Priestess: Solstice is the day when we celebrate the return of the sun. Many early civilizations held festivals celebrating the return of the sun by lighting fires and candles to create as much light as they could. This is known as sympathetic or imaginative magic. It's the belief that imitation can produce the desired effect. The early civilizations believed that "like called to like," that light calls to light, and that lighting fires would cause the sun to come back. Let us, tonight, symbolically bring the return of the light ourselves and honor that amazing phenomenon.

The Dying of the Light

Participant one:
Days are short and nights are cold.
The sun is dying.
Participant one snuffs his/her gold candle.

Participant two:
Time runs on and we grow old.
The sun is dying.
Participant two snuffs his/her gold candle.

Participant three:
Sky is dark
And light is pale.
The sun is dying.
Participant three snuffs his/her gold candle.

Participant four:
We gather in
To no avail
The sun is dying
Participant four snuffs his/her gold candle.

Participant five:
The night is strong
The day is weak
The sun is dying *Participant five snuffs his/her gold candle.*

Participant six:
From the dark
I dare to speak
The sun is dying
Participant six snuffs his/her gold candle.

Participant seven:
I say the words
Of grayest lead
The sun is dead.
Participant seven snuffs his/her gold candle.

Ring bell or chime and listen to fading sound. The only light is the glowing incense burner. We stand in darkness, meditating.

When the silence and darkness have gathered and hearts are quiet, we mediate for a few minutes. After a few minutes of meditation, the priestess quietly touches participant one to signal that she or he should say the next verse.

The Coming of the Light
Participant one:
Again I speak
From utter dark
The light is coming
Participant one uses long match to light candle from incense burner.

Participant two:
A candle flash
Can be the spark
The light is coming
Participant two uses long match to light candle from incense burner.

Participant three:
Hope lives again
In candle glow
The light is coming
Participant three uses long match to light candle from incense burner.

Participant four:
Each new flame
Sees it grow
The light is coming
Participant four uses long match to light candle from incense burner.

Participant five:
Horizon rise
Prophesies
The light is coming
Participant five uses long match to light candle from incense burner.

Participant six:
Look up, look out
Open your eyes
The light is coming
Participant six uses long match to light candle from incense burner.

Participant seven:
I say the words
Of early morn
The sun is born.
Participant seven uses long match to light candle from incense burner.

The Priestess lights the large, gold center candle on the altar.

Bringing in New Light from the Quarters
Participant one leaves the altar and goes to the east candle stand. He or she lights the candle, saying:
I bring new light in from the East.
All: Blessed Be!

Participant two leaves the altar and goes to the south candle stand. He or she lights the candle, saying:
I bring new light in from the South.
All: Blessed Be!

Participant three leaves the altar and goes to the west candle stand. He or she lights the candle, saying:
I bring new light in from the West.
All: Blessed Be!

Participant four leaves the altar and goes to the north candle stand. He or she lights the candle, saying:
I bring new light in from the North.
All: Blessed Be!

Priestess rings bell.
Priestess: The Temple is erected. Let all be here in perfect love and perfect trust.

The Yule Log
Priestess: Let us celebrate the Yule Log.
Yule Elder: Blessed be the tree that gave us this log.
The tree that set its roots in the earth and its branches in the sky.
The tree that drank rain water and danced in the spring breezes
We add our magic to this elemental mix.
Send this power out: tree magic and people magic; earth magic and star magic Send it up over the world to bring light to the world.

Priestess: Let us raise the power.
We hold hands and raise the power. We place hands on the log to imbue the log with our accumulated power. We ground any power left by touching the altar or the floor.

Sharing the Magic
Oak King and Holly King carry the Yule Log to the Fire. All participants follow.
The fire is lit, and the Yule Log is placed on the fire.
If you are using a candle-type Yule log, light the candles instead.

Priestess: May this Yule Log carry our wishes to all who can accept them. *And we return to the altar.*

The Simple Feast

Holly King:

I bless these cakes with the joy of Yule. May we enjoy the sweetness of Yule this night.

Pass the cakes around.

Holly King:

I imbue this cider with the blessing of light. May each day of light be sweet for us all this year coming.

A cup is poured for every participant. Another separate, special cup is poured to honor the Yule Log. The Holly King takes the special cup and throws it on the fire, praising the sun for bringing us warmth and sustenance.

If you are using a candle-type Yule log, sprinkle some wine on the log.

All enjoy cakes and cider contemplatively.

Thanking the Quarters

Participant one leaves the altar and goes to the east candle stand and says:

We thank the spirits of the East for bringing light to this ritual.

The participant on the East extinguishes the candle of the East.

All: Blessed Be!

Participant two leaves the altar and goes to the south candle stand and says:

We thank the spirits of the South for bringing light to this ritual.

The participant on the South extinguishes the candle of the South.

All: Blessed Be!

Participant three leaves the altar and goes to the west candle stand and says:

We thank the spirits of the West for bringing light to this ritual.

The participant on the West extinguishes the candle of the West.

All: Blessed Be!

Participant four leaves the altar and goes to the north candle stand and says:

We thank the spirits of the North for bringing light to this ritual.

The participant on the North extinguishes the candle of the North.

All: Blessed Be!

Opening the Circle
Ring Bell

All: The Circle is open, but unbroken
May the peace of the Goddess go in our hearts
Merry Meet and Merry Part
And Merry Meet again
Blessed Be!

Imbolc

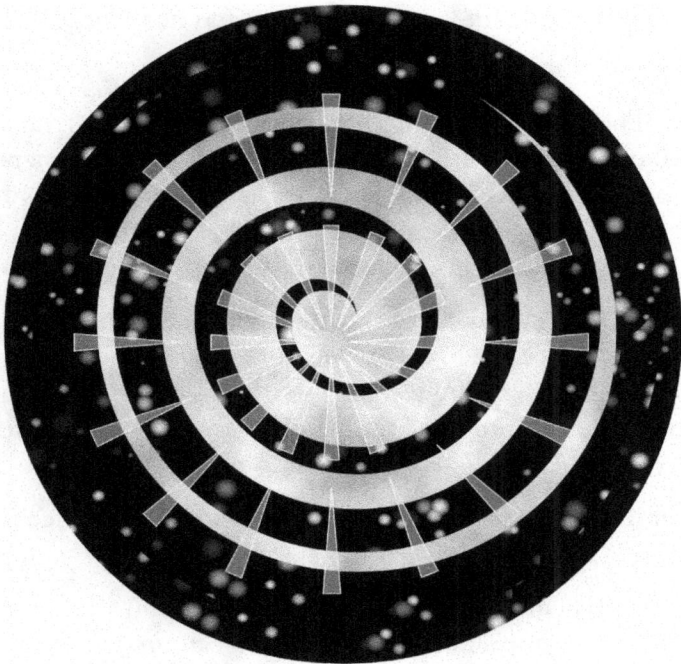

A Glimpse of Infinity

A Ritual of Science and Spirit

A Glimpse of Infinity
Setting up for This Ritual

This ritual could be adapted to any holiday or full moon. It explores the intersection of science and spirituality. The fields of snow and the long winter nights made me think of time and non-time.

Setup

This ritual has a few "stage props." Each participant will need about one yard of wide ribbon and a marker. You also will need a pitcher of water and enough glasses for everyone, as well as the usual four candles for calling the directions, and a bell to begin and end the ritual. All these things should be on the altar at the start of the ritual.

You will need some quieter music for the meditation about 5 to 7 minutes long and some livelier music for the dance – this can be shorter, maybe 3 to 5 minutes. And a space to dance in even if you have to move from the ritual room... and down the hall... through the dining room and back.

Consider having mirrors around the ritual room to enhance the experience.

Part of the ritual involves creating a Mobius strip. A Mobius strip has one side -- it just appears to have two. You can prove this by drawing a line along the strip. Without raising your pen, you will end at the beginning of the line. The purpose of this exercise is to demonstrate the concept of "infinity."

I would suggest that you practice creating a Mobius strip before the ritual and print out the directions below to share with the ritual participants.

You will need someone will need to lead the dance, and one or two people to read the poems, plus the four individuals to call the corners. Arrange who will do what before the ritual starts.

The music for "Round and Round We Go" and for "Go Now in Peace" is available on the internet. Google the whole phrase: "Round and round we go, We hold each other's hands", otherwise you get a different song.

Directions for creating the Mobius strip
1. Start with a long rectangle (ABCD) made of paper, fabric or ribbon.
2. Give the rectangle a half twist.
3. Join the ends so that A is matched with D and B is matched with C.
4. You can now draw a line along the length of the ribbon and without lifting the marker, you can continue the line along both sides of the ribbon. It is a one-sided, unending loop.

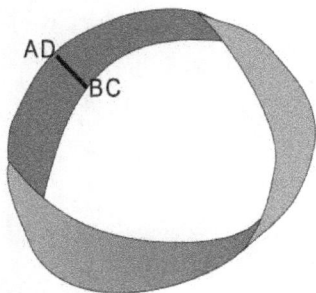

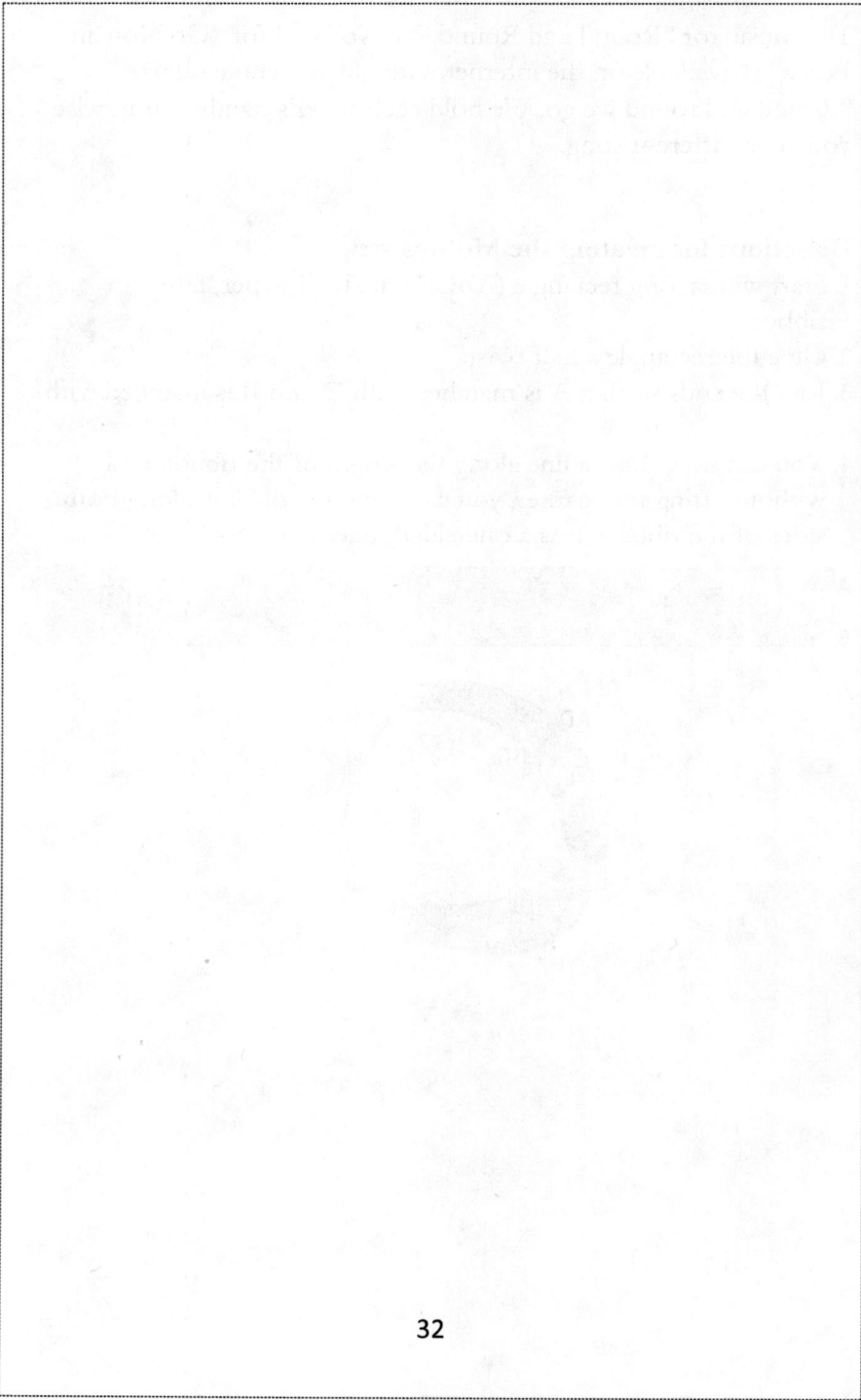

A Glimpse of Infinity
Order of Ritual

We gather around the altar.

Casting the Circle

The Priestess circles the sacred space sweeping it with a broom. First, she moves in a circle to create the space to build the temple, then she moves in a lemniscate (this is a figure eight-shaped curve lying on its side used to symbolize infinity in mathematics).

Calling the Quarters

East Participant: Spirits of the East, Spirits of Air, we call you and invite you to visit with us tonight. Let the winds of the universe speak to us of infinity. *The East participant lights the candle of the East.*
All: Blessed Be.

South Participant: Spirits of the South, Spirits of Fire, we call you and invite you to visit with us tonight. Let the fires of the universe give us the energy of infinity. *The South participant lights the candle of the South.*
All: Blessed Be.

West Participant: Spirits of the West, Spirits of Water, we call you and invite you to visit with us tonight. Let the waters of the universe catch us up in the swirl of infinity. *The West participant lights the candle of the South.*
All: Blessed Be.

North Participant: Spirits of the North, Spirits of Wisdom, we call you and invite you to visit with us tonight. Let the natural world around us show us the patterns of infinity. *The North participant lights the candle of the North.*
All: Blessed Be.

Erecting the Temple

The bell is rung.

Maiden or Priestess: The Temple is erected,
Let all who are within be here in perfect love and perfect trust. Let no anger, evil or mistrust enter within.

An Introduction to the Ritual

Priestess: I wanted to talk about infinity. Perhaps we have all heard about the things I am going to talk about, but I wanted us to use this time to focus on the concept of infinity in a personal and spiritual way.

Infinity is a concept that is hard to hold in our minds. We believe we live in time and space. Since the idea of infinity is outside both of those concepts, it's hard for us to imagine that time may not be linear. Our minds are pattern-making and enumerating machines, while infinity is counter-intuitive and a numberless number. We crave a narrative aspect in our ideas, and infinity is non-narrative. Sometimes, infinity is thought of as a number, a very large number, but this is not really accurate. It is neither large nor small. At point of infinity, numbers are no longer quantitative, but qualitative. As the song Amazing Grace reminds us: When we've been here 10,000 years, bright shining as the sun We've as many days to sing his praise as when we just begun.

That is not the way we usually understand time.

And what about us; how are we infinite? In same way as all of nature. In three dimensions, the earth has limits, but in two dimensions, it does not. You can travel around the world, on the surface infinitely. The universe is limited too. In three dimensions, it is finite, but in four dimensions, perhaps it is not. String theory tells us that in five, six or 11 dimensions, it is definitely infinite.

We have edges, beginnings and endings, we are born and we die... we have limits. In the physical, three-dimensional world, we do indeed have limits. But this is also because we think of ourselves as

34

having a solid form. In other ways, we are infinite. We have the ability to think infinite thoughts, we have an infinite capacity for love, and we each have an infinitely creative nature.

Later in this ritual, we will create Mobius strips and we will see that infinity — or at least its representation can be held in your hand.

I know it is a cliché to quote Blake, but the reason it is a cliché is that no one - no poet, no theologian, no mathematician - could express it better. I read a lot about infinity when researching these ideas, and even physicists quote Blake when trying to explain the concept of infinity.

Therefore, I ask that you please read/listen to this passage by Blake from the Auguries of Innocence— listen to it as though you had not heard it before.
"To see a world in a grain of sand,
And heaven in a wild flower,
Hold infinity in the palm of your hand,
And eternity in an hour."

Today we will do some activities that will remind us of our infinite selves and perhaps, at the end of the ritual, we may be more aware of who we could be.

The Lemniscate Dance
Priestess: The infinity symbol looks like the number eight lying on its side. It is sometimes called the lemniscate, from the Latin lemniscus, meaning "ribbon." I didn't know this when I picked out a physical stand-in for the lemniscate, but in some kind of synchronistic moment, I chose ribbons. Thus, we'll use the ribbons in our dance, and then in a demonstration of the nature of infinity.

We take our ribbons and holding the ribbon of the person in front of us, dance around, following each other to make the shape of the symbol of infinite, the lemniscate.

A Demonstration of Infinity

Priestess: We can create a form of an infinite space with a Möbius strip. A Möbius strip is named after August Ferdinand Möbius, a nineteenth century German mathematician and astronomer, who was a pioneer in the field of topology. You've all seen these strips, in the form of infinity scarves, at least, but I thought it would be a good experience for us to create them.

We create Möbius strips.
Priestess: The proof of the infinite nature of the Möbius strip can be demonstrated by drawing a line down the middle.
Participants draw lines down the middle of the ribbons and prove that the strip has one side — even though it looks as if it has more than one side.

A Meditation on Being an Infinite Spirit

Priestess: Let us place our ribbons on the altar and empower them as symbols of our own infinite natures.
We make a circle of our Möbius strips around the center of the Altar.
We meditate.

Raising the Power of the Infinite

Priestess: Let us raise the power.
We raise the power and send it out.
We ground the power in the Möbius strips.

Song

Priestess: To start the ritual, let us sing about the infinity of the circle of life:
We sing: Round and Round We Go.

Sharing the Basis of Life

Priestess: Let us share water. Water, in its ability to change shape and structure, reminds us of infinity.
The priestess pours glasses of water for each person. As she hands the glass of water to each person she says: I honor the infinite within you. *And the person responds:* Blessed be.

Some Final Words from Rabindranath Tagore

Participant:

On the seashore of endless worlds children meet.
The infinite sky is motionless overhead
And the restless water is boisterous.
On the seashore of endless worlds
The children meet with shouts and dances.
They build their houses with sand,
And they play with empty shells.
With withered leaves they weave
Their boats and smilingly float them
On the vast deep.
Children have their play on the Seashore of worlds.
They know not how to swim,
They know not how to cast nets.
Pearl-fishers dive for pearls,
Merchants sail in their ships,
While children gather pebbles
And scatter them again.
They seek not for hidden treasures,
They know not how to cast nets.
The sea surges up with laughter,
And pale gleams the smile of the sea-beach.
Death-dealing waves sing
Meaningless ballads to the children,
Even like a mother while rocking her baby's cradle.
The sea plays with children,
And pale gleams the smile of the sea-beach.
On the seashore of endless worlds children meet.
Tempest roams in the pathless sky,
Ships are wrecked in the trackless water,
Death is abroad and children play.
On the seashore of endless worlds is the Great meeting of children.

A Closing Song
Sing: Go Now in Peace.

Thanking the Quarters
Priestess: As we mention each of the elements, think on how each of these shows us the patterns of chaos, the visual representation of infinity.

East Participant: Spirits of the East, Spirits of Air, we thank you for the restless winds that endlessly blow around the earth.
East Participant extinguishes the candle of the East.

South Participant: Spirits of the South, Spirits of Fire, we thank you for the dancing, changing flames.
South Participant extinguishes the candle of the East.

West Participant: Spirits of the West, Spirits of Water, we thank you for the swirling, encircling waters.
West Participant extinguishes the candle of the East.

North Participant: Spirits of the North, Spirits of Earth, we thank you for the complexity of reality.
North Participant extinguishes the candle of the East.

Ending Prayer
The bell is rung.
All: The Circle is open but unbroken
May the peace of The Goddess go in our hearts
Merry Meet and Merry Part
And Merry Meet again
Blessed Be!

Ostara

New Winds & New Ideas

New Winds & New Ideas
Setting up for This Ritual

Ostara, also called Eostar, is about new life, and eggs are one of the traditional symbols of this holiday. This ritual uses eggs in the way symbols are supposed to be used. Symbols should stand as reminders of concepts that are hard to verbalize. For example, I like using a broom for Spring Equinox and Imbolc. It's symbolic of newness and cleanliness.

Setup Equipment:
You will need four eggs per person: one each in yellow, red, blue and green. You can use hardboiled real eggs, or plastic or wooden eggs. Each option changes the ritual a little. If the eggs open, like plastic eggs, the strips of paper can be put in the eggs. If the eggs are hardboiled or solid wood, you can write on the eggs. If you are using real eggs, participants might want to assemble early and have a community egg dye.

Put the eggs on the altar along with slips of paper (if using plastic eggs) and a felt-tip pen for each participant. At the end of the ritual, you will need one small basket for each person.

The altar should also have bread and wine, or cakes and juice for the simple feast. Egg bread or cookies shaped like eggs would be appropriate.

The cardinal compass points are used twice: one to call the quarters and once to bless the eggs. One group of four people can do both, or you may use two groups, depending on how many people attend. One or perhaps two people will be needed to bless the bread and wine.

You will need four short recorded musical pieces that are about three to five minutes in length. These should be appropriate for meditation, so natural sounds or spa music would work. There is a sharing of ideas after each egg rite. However, it's not mandatory to share ideas, and I don't think anyone should be forced to share.

New Winds and New Ideas
Order of Ritual

Casting the circle

The priestess sweeps the perimeter of circle three times.

Priestess: I clear the circle of the old, I raise the temple of the new. I see around me the shining temple.

Calling the quarters

Participant: We call the winds of the East, if they be willing to attend us. We welcome now the breezes of spring, opening our minds to new ideas. May the Eastern breezes enhance our thinking processes and blow away old ways of thinking.

Light the candle of the East.

All: Blessed be!

Participant: We call the winds of the South, if they be willing to attend us. We anticipate the warmth of the summer air. May the winds of the South strengthen us and burn away old ideas that are hampering our growth.

Light the candle of the South.

All: Blessed be!

Participant: We call the winds of the West, if they be willing to attend us. The cool winds of autumn speak of seasons past and hold the serenity of continuity. Let our new ideas carry the good things of past concepts even as we move beyond them.

Light the candle of the West.

All: Blessed be!

Participant: We call the winds of the North, if they be willing to attend us. Even as we say good-bye to winter, the sharpness of the winter wind keeps us alert. The wisdom of the earth is carried on the winter wind and if we want to be wise, we will listen to it.

Light the candle of the North.

All: Blessed be!

Introduction to the Ritual
Priestess: We celebrate the newness of spring by spending some time trying to think new thoughts.

The winds of spring blow through our minds bringing fresh ideas and new ways of looking at life. Eggs are a traditional symbol of newness. Colors also have traditional symbolic meanings. This ritual brings together these symbols as a way of triggering ideas.

New Idea Egg:
Participant standing in the East: Yellow is the color of the East and the intellect. It is the dawn and a symbol of beginnings. We start now to exercise our minds anew.

Priestess: Pick up your yellow egg and hold it. We will spend a few minutes thinking about something new that we want to learn — this could be on any topic that is of interest to you. Now, think about how you would learn about that new thing and what other paths it might lead you down. Write down your topic *(either on the eggs or on the strips of paper)* and place it in the yellow egg *(if you are using plastic eggs)* and then put the egg in the basket.
Play music and meditate.
After meditation and writing notes, there is a group sharing of ideas.
Priestess: If you wish to share your idea with us, please tell us.

New Action Egg
Participant standing in the South: Red is the color of the South and of the physical body. It is the hot sun of noon and the symbol of action.

Priestess: Pick up your red egg and hold it. We will spend a few minutes thinking about our bodies and about a new activity, doing something for our bodies — or with our bodies. Perhaps we consider something as frivolous as a new hair color, or we think of something fun such as rock climbing. We could also think of something serious like getting a physical that you have been putting off. Now, think

about how it will feel to be in your body while doing this activity. Write down how you feel about what you are considering doing *(either on the eggs or on the strips of paper)* and place it in the red egg *(if you are using plastic eggs)* and then place the egg in the basket.
Play music and meditate.
After meditation and writing notes, there is a group sharing of ideas.
Priestess: If you wish to share your idea with us, please tell us.

New Emotions Egg

Participant standing in the West: Blue is the color of the west and of emotional life It is the coolness of evening and the symbol of tranquility.

Priestess: Pick up your blue egg and hold it. Think about an unresolved emotional situation you have and see if you can think of a way to alleviate it. Or perhaps meditate on a good emotional situation and resolve to be appreciative of it in the future. Think about how this will make you feel and see if this will move you toward serenity. Write down this experience *(either on the eggs or on the strips of paper)* and place it in the blue egg *(if you are using plastic eggs)* and then place the egg in the basket.
Play music and meditate.
After meditation and writing notes, there is a group sharing of ideas.
Priestess: If you wish to share your idea with us, please tell us.

Mother Earth Egg

Participant standing in the North: Green is the color of Mother Earth. In this time, when we celebrate the spring and the earth again covers herself with the beauty of leaves and flowers, it is appropriate to contemplate the wonder of the earth's gifts -- that all of our sustenance comes from the earth. All that we are and all that we have comes from her.

Priestess: Pick up your green egg and hold it. Think of something you can do for Mother Earth and her other inhabitants, like planting a tree or switching to earth-friendly detergent or volunteering at an animal shelter. Resolve to move forward in your thinking about

living lightly on the earth. Write down this idea *(either on the eggs or on the strips of paper)* and place it in the green egg *(if you are using plastic eggs)* and then place the egg in the basket.
Play music and meditate.
After meditation and writing notes, there is a group sharing of ideas.
Priestess: If you wish to share your idea with us, please tell us.

Ceremony of the Simple Feast
Priestess: In celebration of what the earth gives us, we eat and drink now in conscious appreciation of all that we have.

The Priestess or a participant blesses the bread or cookies and passes the plate around. (Blessing should be spontaneous.)
All: Blessed be!
The Priestess or a participant blesses the wine or cider and passes the cups around. (Blessing should be spontaneous.)
All: Blessed be!

Thanking the Winds
Participant: We thank now the spirits of the winds, mindful of all the newness they have brought us. We thank the spirits of the East for new thoughts we now hold.
Extinguish the candle of the East.
All: Blessed be!

Participant: We thank the spirits of the South for the new actions we will now undertake.
Extinguish the candle of the South.
All: Blessed be!

We thank the spirits of the West for the new path to tranquility we now walk.
Extinguish the candle of the West.
All: Blessed be!

We thank the spirits of the North for the earth who brings us understanding of the oneness of nature.

Extinguish the candle of the North.
All: Blessed be!

Priestess: We feel renewed in our thinking, our actions, our loving kindness and our understanding. We walk now the path of life in joy and thoughtfulness.

Opening the circle
Ring Bell.
All: The Circle is open, but unbroken
May the peace of the Goddess go in our hearts
Merry Meet and Merry Part
And Merry Meet again
Blessed Be!

Beltane

A Joyful Life
An Urban Beltane Ritual

A Joyful Life
Setting up for This Ritual

Traditionally, Mayday rituals involved dancing around a maypole. But, if you live in an urban area, a backyard or other area for a Maypole may not be available. This ritual gives the urban pagan a chance to celebrate a traditional Mayday indoors or on a patio. You will still need enough space for the participants to walk around the altar.

Here's how I made a "tabletop" Maypole. I nailed a 24" dowel to the center of a wooden disk (both available at Michael's). I put the dowel and disk in a bucket and filled the bucket with sand. I hot-glued 1/4" ribbons, all different colors, to the top of the dowel. Be sure you have at least as many ribbons as participants.

The maypole ritual includes a toast to Mother Nature, so the ritual calls for a tree that the participants can gather around. I have used a mini-apple tree in the past, but any potted plant can represent Mother Nature. Depending on the size, you may want to put this on a second altar or move the maypole after the first part of the ritual and replace it with the plant. If it is large enough, it can be on the floor. You could also move the gathering outside for this part of the ritual.

I like to have candles set at the perimeter of the circle for this ritual. If you are having the directional candles on the altar, use flameless electronic candles so you don't set fire to the ribbons during the dance.

Roles for this ritual include callers for the corners, someone to bless the May wine, someone to read the poem, and optionally, someone to kindle the fire. Write to the participants beforehand. They will want to know about the tree blessings and if you are having the bonfire, the fire blessings. They will also need to know about the songs: *We Circle Around* and *Louis Armstrong's Wonderful World*. Music for both songs are available on the internet.

The traditional garb for this event is a white dress or robe and a flower crown. I have made the flower crowns, either by using live branches of flowering trees or by using silk flowers. I find that men participants prefer leafy crowns to the flower ones, so I usually create those as well. On occasion, I have also asked folks to come early and make their own crowns. This does lengthen an already long ritual, but it is very enjoyable.

A Joyful Dance
Order of Ritual

Clearing the Circle
The Priestess walks the circle, marking the circle with incense or sweeping with a broom
Priestess: I clear this space of all negativity and bad feelings. I bless this time and this space for a ritual of spirit. Let no anger, hate or jealousy enter here. Here let only friendship be in perfect love and perfect trust.

Calling the Corners
Participant in the East: I call the spirits of the East, the spirits of new life. Let us feel the breeze on our faces and know the joy of the spring.
Light the candle in the East.
All: Blessed Be!

Participant in the South: I call the spirits of the South, the spirits of the returning sun. Let us feel the warm sun on our faces and experience the joy of the spring.
Light the candle in the South.
All: Blessed Be!

Participant in the West: I call the spirits of the West, the spirits of gentle spring rain. Let us feel the soft spring rain on our faces and feel the joy of the spring.
Light the candle in the West.
All: Blessed Be!

Participant in the North: I call the spirits of the North, the spirits of the earth in bloom. Let us feel the spirit of endless renewal in our beings and truly understand the joy of the spring.
Light the candle in the North.
All: Blessed Be!

Raising the Temple

Priestess: We set this time and place aside for ritual.
In this place that is no place and that is all places
In this time that is no time and that is all time
We stand between the worlds.
Ring bell.
The temple is erected, let all who are here, be here in peace and love.

An Explanation of the Ritual

Priestess: May Day! Beltane! The irrepressible holiday! Generations of Christians tried to stomp it out, trying to push a dark view of a life of restraint over a raucous, life-affirming, sexually free day of unrestrained joy. People all over Europe still celebrate May Day, although it may be with fewer sexual overtones than in pre-Christian days. It's important to celebrate our bodies and being alive — the wonder of being able to dance and sing, to run, to make love. It's the gift that makes everything else possible. We often admire our own intellect and celebrate our emotional life, but we don't often honor our bodies, when having a body is the very definition of life.

So today, we come together to honor the dance of life as represented by the maypole, to sing joyfully, to enjoy the spring and mostly to remind ourselves that our bodies are the essence of our selfness.

A Joyful Dance
Priestess: Kipling says:
"Oh, do not tell the Priest of our plight,
Or he would call it sin;
But we shall be out in the woods all night,
Aconjuring summer in!
And we bring you news by word of mouth
For women, cattle and corn
Now is the dun come up from the South
With Oak, and Ash and Thorn!

The Colors of Life

Priestess: Let us each select a ribbon taking a color that reflects something meaningful to us.
Participants each select a ribbon. Any ribbons not selected can be left to hang or taken up as a second ribbon by one of the participants.

The Joyful Dance

We circle the mini maypole, chanting
We circle around, we circle around
The boundaries of the earth
We circle around, we circle around
The boundaries of the Earth
Wearing our long wing feathers as we fly
Wearing our long wing feathers as we fly
We circle around, we circle around
The boundaries of the sky*

(Repeat until the ribbons have reached the bottom of the "pole") The priestess ties the ribbons together at the base of the "pole".

All: Blessed be!

A Toast to Mother Earth

Priestess: Let us honor a plant of Mother Earth's creation.
We proceed to the selected tree or place the "tree" on the altar.

Blessing the wine

Participant: I bless this wine as a symbol of the sweetness of the spring and the joy we find in it. *All: Blessed Be!*
He or she pours a cup of May wine for each participant.

Each participant in turn says a blessing for the earth.
(Ideas for Blessings:
Participant: May the earth remind us of beauty when we see the May flowers or
Participant: May the spring breezes raise our spirits or
Participant: May we lift our heads and smile when we hear birdsong.

Or whatever the participant is inspired to say.)
All: Blessed Be!
Each participant splashes a drop or two on the tree and then drinks the rest.

Song: *We sing Louis Armstrong's Wonderful World.*

Participant reads:
A Closing Poem by Walt Whitman

We two—how long we were fool'd!
Now transmuted, we swiftly escape, as Nature escapes;
We are Nature—long have we been absent, but now we return;
We become plants, leaves, foliage, roots, bark;
We are bedded in the ground — we are rocks;
We are oaks — we grow in the openings side by side;
We browse — we are two among the wild herds, spontaneous as any;
We are two fishes swimming in the sea together;
We are what the locust blossoms are—we drop scent around the
lanes, mornings and evenings;
We are also the coarse smut of beasts, vegetables, minerals;
We are two predatory hawks — we soar above, and look down;
We are two resplendent suns — we it is who balance ourselves,
orbic and stellar -- we are as two comets;
We prowl fang'd and four-footed in the woods — we spring on prey;
We are two clouds, forenoons and afternoons, driving overhead;
We are seas mingling —
we are two of those cheerful waves, rolling over each other, and
interwetting each other;
We are what the atmosphere is, transparent, receptive, pervious,
impervious:
We are snow, rain, cold, darkness —
we are each product and influence of the globe;
We have circled and circled till we have arrived home again —
we two have;
We have voided all but freedom, and all but our own joy.

Thanking the Quarters

Participant in the East: We thank the spirits of the East who bring us flowers and music.
The participant in the East extinguishes the candle of the East.
All: Blessed Be!

Participant in the South: We thank the spirits of the South who bring us the returning sunshine.
The participant in the South extinguishes the candle of the South.
All: Blessed Be!

Participant in the West: We thank the spirits of the West who bring us spring showers.
The participant in the West extinguishes the candle of the West.
All: Blessed Be!

Participant in the North: We thank the spirits of the North who bring us the wonderful tree we blessed and that we took blessings from.
The participant in the North extinguishes the candle of the North.
All: Blessed Be!

Opening the Circle

Ring Bell
All: The Circle is Open, but Unbroken
May the peace of the Goddess go in our hearts
Merry Meet and Merry Part And Merry Meet Again
Blessed Be!

Litha

The Flower Mandala
A Ritual of Meditation

The Flower Mandala
Setting up for This Ritual

For the ritual, you need the components of the mandala - petals, leaves, herbs, small flowers. I have an herb garden and the thyme was in bloom, so I cut small sprigs of thyme and some lemon balm leaves. I cut some small leaves from a hawthorn shrub and from my miniature roses. I also bought 2 bouquets at the supermarket. From these I got alstroemeria, daisies and roses and a sunflower. I cut stems off the alstroemeria and daisies, the petals off the roses and saved the sunflower for the center of the mandala. Other participants brought nasturtiums, ivy, snapdragons, and honeysuckle, both blossoms and leaves.

For the base, I drew a 24-inch circle on a piece of black felt. I used felt because things placed on felt tend to stay in place. I used a stiff piece of cardboard under the felt. I had 2 altars, one with the ritual tools and one with just the felt cover, ready for the mandala. The directional candles were set at the perimeter of the ritual circle (not on either altar).

Basically, you only need the flowers and a base to build the mandala, along with the sheet music for the songs and perhaps some recorded music for the meditation.

We also have done this ritual with seashells in place of flowers, at the beach, which was fun. That time, someone blew a conch shell to start and end the ritual instead of a bell.

The music for "Round and Round We Go" and for "DeColores" is available on the internet. Google the whole phrase:
"Round and round we go, We hold each other's hands", otherwise you get a different song.

The Flower Mandala
Order of Ritual

We gather around the altar.

Casting the Circle
The Priestess circles the sacred space three times carrying a sunflower. She returns to the north of the circle and states: In this time that is no time and in this place that is not place, I set this circle outside time and space for a ritual of spirit.

Calling the Corners
East Participant: I call the winds of the east, recalling to us the blooms of spring and the lightness of the spring spirit.
Light the candle of the East.
All: Blessed Be!

South Participant: I call the winds of the south, reminding us of the ripening of fruit and the brightness of summer spirit.
Light the candle of the South.
All: Blessed Be!

West Participant: I call the winds of the west, the forthcoming time of harvest and the appreciative soul.
Light the candle of the West.
All: Blessed Be!

North Participant: I call the winds of the north, the time of austere beauty and contemplative spirit.
Light the candle of the North.
All: Blessed Be!

Erecting the Temple
The bell is rung.
Maiden or Priestess: The Temple is erected,

Let all who are within be here in perfect love and perfect trust. Let no anger, evil or mistrust enter within.

An Introduction to the Ritual
Priestess: This year, our ritual for Litha involves creating a flower-leaf mandala. The symbolic activity brings together all the symbols of the holiday and of ritual. Mandalas are circular and radiant, like the sun. The sun is the catalyst for plant growth and flower blossoms.

This time of year, the sun brings the world of vegetation into glorious abundance. We are dependent on this world, but modern life keeps us separated from it. We are blind to its beauty. We spend our lives indoors staring at screens. Or we are rushing somewhere in a car, watching the traffic, perhaps to get to an office, which may not even have windows. Building a mandala will allow us to focus on the details of the leaves and flowers we are using. They will become real to us, not a blur of green on the other side of the car's windows.

And why a circle? If all the symbols for all the holidays were reduced to simple shapes, my choice for Litha would be the circle. Litha is a celebration of the sun, which brings us the cycle of the seasons, the wheel of the year and the circle of life. A mandala is a perfect analog for these solar realities.

We will build our mandala and then maybe our meditation of the mandala will bring the energy of the sun to us -- to enlighten us, to brighten our lives, to energize our actions.

Song
Priestess: To bring the us into the center of the ritual spirit, we'll sing Round and Round We Go.
Sing Round and Round we Go

Building the Flower Mandala
Priestess: Taking turns, we choose our materials and create a mandala. Let the design bring us to find our calm center. *Priestess removes the stem from the sunflower and places the sunflower at the center of the*

mandala. The participant to her left makes a small circle of petals or leaves around the sunflower. The next participant makes a second circle around the first. The participants continue making concentric circles until the entire area is filled.

Meditation
Priestess: Focusing now on our mandala, ground and center. Enter into a state of calmness and awareness. *We meditate, perhaps to recorded music or water sounds.*

Raising the Power *Priestess:*
Let us join our power together.
A cone of power is raised. When the power is peaked, the participants raise their hands to send the power to any who need it and can accept it. Any extra is grounded by touching the ground. A moment of silence is observed.
Priestess: Let us send out power to those who need it and can accept it.

A Closing Song
Sing DeColores

Thanking the Quarters
East Participant:
We thank the spirits of the east and bless them for the gift of flowers. Extinguish the Candle of the East.

South Participant:
We thank the spirits of the south and bless them for the gift of greens. *Extinguish the Candle of the South.*

West Participant:
We thank the spirits of the west and bless them for the gift of the harvest. *Extinguish the Candle of the West.*

North Participant:
We thank the spirits of the north and bless them for the gift of harmony. *Extinguish the Candle of the North.*

Ending Prayer

The bell is rung.

All: The Circle is open but unbroken
May the peace of The Goddess
go in our hearts
Merry Meet and Merry Part
And Merry Meet again
Blessed Be!

Lammas

The Great Alchemy
Four Elements Create the Harvest

The Great Alchemy
Setting up for This Ritual

Lammas is the festival of the first harvest, the celebration of grain. It is a time of great feasting. This ritual celebrates the four North-American foods most representative of this time of year. It also celebrates nature as she skillfully conjures food from wind, sun, rain and soil.

This ritual is subtitled "Four Elements Create the Harvest." It's a moment to stop and consider how the foods we eat are created by the magic combination of air, sun, water and the good earth under our feet.

This is one of the simpler rituals to set up. The ritual only requires a small dish of cooked corn (from a fresh ear), a cut up tomato, some cubes of watermelon and a cooked potato also cut into cubes. Enough of each vegetable is needed for everyone to have a bite. And everyone will need a spoon or a fork and a napkin.

The altar should be decorated with sunflowers, decorations of wheat and corn along with fresh bread. Four candles should be set at the four cardinal directions. You will need a short piece of music for the meditation.

Roles for this ritual include four people for the directions. The directions are used twice: To call the corners and to honor the elements of the harvest, so four or eight participants could be involved in these parts of the ritual.

The music for the ritual, Dona Nobis Pacem can be found on the internet. If you practice, you can sing it as a round and it is uplifting!

The Great Alchemy
Order of Ritual

Opening Ceremony - Presentation of the Harvest

The participants, except for the Priestess, gather at the altar.

The Priestess approaches the altar, carrying a tray with plates of corn, tomato, watermelon and potato.
She presents the tray to the person of the East, who takes the corn and puts on the altar.
East Participant: Corn I place in the East to honor the wind.
All: Blessed Be!

She presents the tray to the person of the South, who takes the tomato and puts on the altar.
South Participant: Tomato I place in the South to honor the sun.
All: Blessed Be!

She presents the tray to the person of the West, who takes the watermelon and puts on the altar.
West Participant: Watermelon I place in the West to honor the rain.
All: Blessed Be!

She presents the tray to the person of the North, who takes the potato and puts on the altar.
North Participant: Potato I place in the North to honor the soil.
All: Blessed Be!

Casting the Circle

The Priestess circles the sacred space, defining it with a sword to cut it apart.
Priestess: I clear this space of all negativity and bad feelings. I bless this time and this space for a ritual of spirit. Let no anger, hate or jealousy enter here. Here let only friendship be.

Call to the Four Elements

East participant lights the candle of the East:

Spirits of the East, spirits of air, we call you and invite you to visit with us tonight.
We call the spirit of the winds that pollinate the grain.
We call the spirit of sky, so full of bees and butterflies that pollinate the fruit.
We call the spirit of air that brings us the breath of life, for us and the plants we harvest.
We call the spirits of oxygen and carbon dioxide to breathe, and nitrogen to grow green.
On this day that we celebrate life, we celebrate the air that brings us life.
All: Blessed Be!

South participant lights the candle of the South:
Spirits of the South, spirits of fire, we call you and invite you to visit with us tonight.
We call the spirit of summer which sends warmth to the earth for growth.
We call the spirit of the fiery sun that ripens our harvest.
We call the spirit of solar energy that fuels the plant growth to bring us the harvest, to sustain us. On this day that we celebrate life, we celebrate the fire that brings us life.
All: Blessed Be!

West Participant lights the candle of the West:
Spirits of the West, spirits of water, we call you and invite you to visit with us tonight.
We call the spirit of blessed rain to start germination.
We call the spirit of water that nurtures the crop.
We call the spirit of water filling the cells of the stems and the leaves, Nourishing and sustaining, supporting and strengthening.
On this day that we celebrate life, we celebrate the water that brings us life.
All: Blessed Be!

North Participant lights the candle of the North:

Spirits of the North, spirits of the earth, we call you and invite you to visit with us tonight.
We call the spirit of the fertile earth that is our mother.
We call the spirit of she who brings forth the plants to feed us.
We call the spirit of the rocks, the soil, the cycle of decay and rebirth.
All of these are the gifts of the earth for us
From the worms, to the trees, to ourselves -- all are part of the living matrix that is Gaia, Planet Earth
We honor her tonight, at the time of harvest.
On this day that we celebrate life, we celebrate the earth that brings us life.
All: Blessed Be!

Erecting the Temple
Ring bell.
Priestess: The Temple is erected,
Let all who are within it be here in perfect love and perfect trust. Let no anger, evil or mistrust enter within.

An Introduction to the Ritual
Priestess: Now is Lammas, first harvest, a time of the fullness of grain. In the Irish tradition, it is the festival of Lughnasadh, when Lugh, the Sun God is honored. It is the time of gratitude for what we are just beginning to receive. This is a time when we give thanks for the results of sowing crops in anticipation of eventual harvest — projects which were begun long ago. We look across our gardens and see what our work, together with sun, air, water and soil, has brought us. Perhaps we look also at other projects, endeavors begun long ago that are now coming to fruition.

It is time when everything seems full. The days are full of sun and heat, the fields are full and ready for harvest, the air is full of bees and butterflies. Even so, we know that the days are waning, the shadows grow longer; the peak of the sun's powers are past. Summer is dying, his power is being siphoned into the corn. The Goddess turns the wheel of life and the seasons change. The oak king begins his journey to relinquish his crown; his journey that ends at Samhain.

But for now, the days are still long, the berries are sweet and the harvest gives us the hope of a comfortable winter. We celebrate the fulfillment of life on Lammas.

Honoring the Gifts of the Earth

Priestess: We now honor the gifts of the earth to us and share them as a circle, since the gifts of the earth are given to all and fellowship is one of those gifts. No harvest comes to the table without shared effort. No harvest should be celebrated without sharing the love and friendship it represents.

East Participant: I honor the wind. Since all grain is wind-pollinated, without the wind, we would have no grain. Grain is the sustainer of mankind. Community life, and thus civilization, is based on grain. Each society has a characteristic grain that represents that culture. In the Americas, the traditional sustenance of life is corn.

By pausing in our year's journey to salute the grain, corn, we honor the wind that pollinates each strand of corn silk, one grain of pollen sliding down to fertilize a single kernel, more than a billion times each year.

Priestess: We now share the magic of the wind.
The East participant passes the corn around. We all eat and focus on the corn as we eat.

South Participant: I honor the sun. Tomatoes so directly mirror the sun in miniature. Great glowing globes of red and yellow — of all the vegetables, the sun-worshiper — unhappy and green until the heat of high summer kisses it, ripens it; completes it. We pause to salute the tomato, the creation of the sun!

Priestess: We now share the magic of the sunshine.
The South participant passes the chopped tomato around so that each participant can take a small portion. We all eat and focus on the tomato as we eat.

West Participant: I honor the water. Watermelon, the plant named for this element; the fruit of memories of happy summer days and childhood picnics. We pause to remember the sweetness of summer and its fruits.

Water IS the harvest because the plants of the harvest are mostly cellulose-enclosed water. In the plants, we sense the rains of springs and the summer showers that bring us the harvest. We pause to salute the watermelon, the creation of water.

Priestess: We now share the magic of the water.
The West participant passes the cut-up melon around so that each person can have a small portion. We all eat and focus on the melon as we eat.

North Participant: I honor the earth. North is the seat of Gaia, the great earth mother. No plant grown is as earthy as the potato — the basic staple food for millions. Soil and potatoes are intimately tied together. Mound the good earth on the potato plant as it grows. The more earth, the more potatoes. We pause to salute the potato…the strength of our mother earth, in compact form!

Priestess: We now share the magic of the soil.
The West participant passes the potato around. We all eat and focus on the potato as we eat.

Meditation
Priestess: Let us now hold hands and meditate on the gifts of the earth and the gift of shared pleasures. Let us meditate on what we have accomplished and what we have to look forward to. In this time, we harvest that which we have planted from the seeds of our previous harvest. And we save some of the seeds from this current harvest for next spring to begin the cycle again. There is no end which does not ultimately lead to a beginning, nor any beginning which does not ultimately lead to an end
Play Music.
Meditate on what we have eaten and what it means.

Raising the Power

Priestess: Let us raise the power for our future endeavors and with the hope of more harvests. *We raise the power.*

The Great Alchemy

Let us send energy out to all our loved ones and all whom have a need for help.

We raise our arms and send out the power.

Let us ground the power.

We touch the altar or the ground.

Closing Thoughts

Priestess: This circle of life is a ponderable wonder — this pattern that weaves food for us from the nitrogen and carbon dioxide of the air, the water from the sky, the minerals in the soil and powers the process with sunlight. The plants produce energy in an easily stored form. They save with that energy a tiny replica of themselves – in the form of seeds. Some of that stored energy we use for food. But we save some of those tiny seed-selves that each plant creates to save the plant's energy over the winter. Those are protected by us during the winter and planted in the spring, turning the wheel once more. The cooperative system that we have worked out with the plants over the millennia still sustains us. The complex interweaving of life forces on earth still amazes us.

Ending Song

We sing Dona Nobis Pacem

Thanking the Elements

The participant extinguishes the candle in the East, saying:

Participant: We thank the spirits of the east, who remind us of the part that air and wind weave in the pattern of life.

All: Blessed be.

The participant extinguishes the candle in the South, saying:

Participant: We thank the spirits of the South, who remind us of the part that heat and light weave in the pattern of life.
All: Blessed be.

The participant extinguishes the candle in the West, saying:
Participant: We thank the spirits of the West, who remind us of the part that rain and water weave in the pattern of life.
All: Blessed be.

The participant extinguishes the candle in the North, saying:
Participant: We thank the spirits of the North, who remind us of the part that the sustaining, nurturing, and beautiful earth weaves in the pattern of life.
All: Blessed be.

Opening the Circle
All: The circle is open, but unbroken
May the peace of the Goddess go in our hearts
Merry Meet and Merry Part
And Merry Meet Again.

Blessed Be!

Mabon

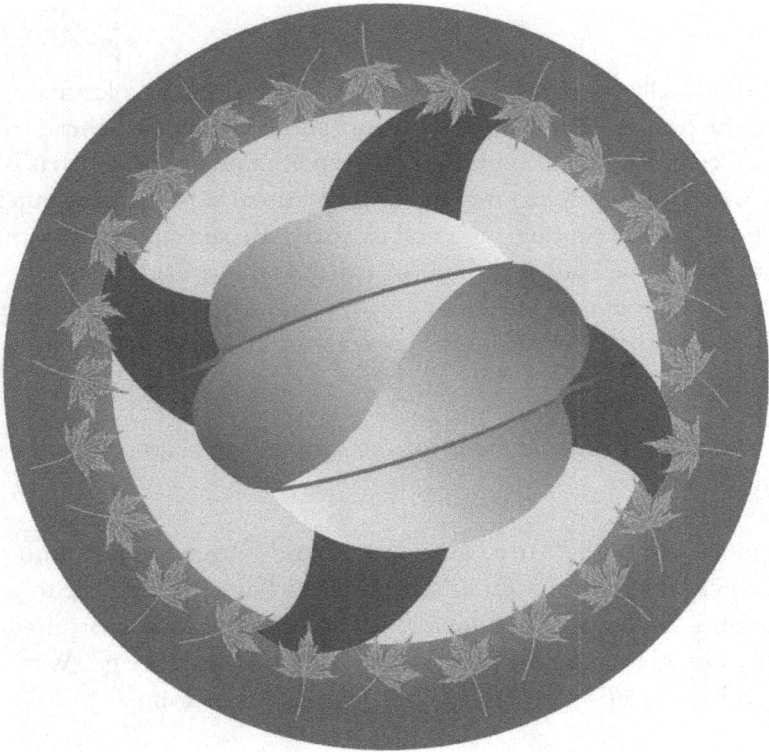

Accepting Change

Accepting Change
Setting up for This Ritual

Many of us find change difficult, even pleasant changes. This ritual is designed to open our minds to change and accept the changes that come to us. Life is all about change. Even rocks change.

Setup
This ritual calls for at least one potato per person, plus a knife to carve the potato with. The participants should be alerted ahead of time in case they wish to bring their own athame or boline (that is, their own ritual knife) to the ritual. If the ritual is performed outside, you need a small pit dug, with soil to cover. Be sure to dig your pit where no one will fall in during the ritual. If the ritual is inside, a bucket or planter is needed along with some soil to cover. In both cases, a trowel or a small shovel is necessary to cover the potatoes with soil.

You will need bread and cider for the simple feast, along with glasses for the cider.

The music for both "Turn, Turn, Turn" and "Round and Round we go" is available on the web. It's also nice to have some music to play during the meditation. Nature sounds are good or quiet instrumental music. Google the whole phrase: "Round and round we go, We hold each other's hands", otherwise you get a different song.

Roles for this ritual include the four directions and someone to read the poem. The reader should get the poem ahead of time, since it is fairly long.

Accepting Change
Order of Ritual

Casting the circle
The Priestess walks the circle with a candle.
Priestess: I set aside this place and this time for a ritual of spirit.

Invoking the Spirits of the Wind
East Participant: Lighting the East candle, says: I salute the winds of the East, the winds of change and newness. May we be open to you this night.
All: Blessed Be!

South Participant: lighting the South candle, says: I salute the winds of the South, the winds of strength and passion. May we be decisive this night.
All: Blessed Be!

West Participant: lighting the West candle, says: I salute the winds of the West, the winds of empathy and affection. May we be understanding of ourselves this night.
All: Blessed Be!

North Participant: lighting the North candle, says: I salute the winds of the North, the winds of stability. May we understand that stability requires change.
All: Blessed Be!

We return to the center of the circle. Ring bell.
Priestess: The Temple is erected. Let all who are here be here of their free will, with love and trust.

An Introduction to the Ritual
Tonight is the night of the changing of seasons, when the cool winds of autumn replace the hot air of the summer. It is a time when the leaves cast off their green colors and show us their brilliant reds and

yellows. It is a time when we see a clear blue morning sky, rather than the hazy overheated summer sky.

Yet, we are uneasy with this change, because these changes foreshadow the coming of winter, the cold, wet, isolating winter. We anticipate this change with fear and discomfort. This clouds our ability to revel in what autumn brings – the wonder of the harvest's gifts to us; the blessing of weather that is neither too hot nor too cold; the beauty of rain that does not have the violence of summer lightening nor winter blizzards.

Change is often mirrored in other aspects of our lives; change is uncomfortable. Some changes are inevitable, and some are by choice. All of them carry risk and the fear of the unknown. And, it is in our nature to be uneasy and to resist change. Some changes lead to a better self, some changes do not, but still, changes are inevitable. Some changes can be viewed in many ways, as having aspects that are desirable, even if initially unwanted. Some changes are completely disheartening and no good can come of them, but we must still accept them.

But some unwelcome changes carry the seeds of something we want very badly, and that change is the passage that will get us the reward that we have been seeking. For example, we may not want the cold weather, but we cannot have apples in fall without cold in the winter. The trees may bloom in the spring, but the apples will not develop.

Accepting Change

Tonight, as the leaves turn, we turn inward to seek guidance in embracing the changes that take place both within our beings and outside of ourselves. We cannot control all aspects of the world around us. We cannot always control what our bodies are doing, even while we are living in those bodies. For instance, sometimes our minds have a tendency to wander off without us as we daydream in a class or at work. Tonight, we seek to understand that accepting change is part of what makes us human. Change can also help us to evolve spiritually; perhaps become transcendent.

Song
Sing Round and Round We Go.

The Power Potato
Each participant reaches into the basket and chooses a potato.
Priestess: There are many stages in the process of change. Sometimes we need to shed old ways to start the process of change. Sometimes we have been through the process of growth and change and we simply need to accept that it has happened. Sometimes we are ignoring a change that is currently in process.

Priestess: Let us tonight lose those things that are blocking us from changing and from accepting change.
We carve symbols that are meaningful to ourselves or just symbolic openings in our potatoes.
Let us now fill these symbolic vessels with our feelings of conflict, blockage and fear.
We hold our potatoes and meditate for five or 10 minutes while music plays. We channel our negative energy into the potatoes.

Priestess: When we are ready, let us each bury our potatoes and with them all the things that keep us from entering into change, recognizing it, and accepting it.
One-by-one, we bury our potatoes.

Raising the Power
Priestess: Now that we are emptied of negative energy, let us raise our positive power. Once it raised, let us send it out to those who need it and can accept it with joy.
Holding hands, we raise the power, send it out and ground it in the potato pit or pot.

Song
Sing Turn, Turn, Turn

The Simple Feast
Priestess: This is also a harvest festival and we take time tonight to honor the changes the plants go through in order to bring us the means by which we live.

Priestess or Participant holding the bread: This is the bread of life made from the wheat of the fields. From seeds shown this spring, this wheat grew to a tall green plant, transforming over the season to the gold of summer. It was cut down and its long stalks were no longer rooted in the earth. It was gathered and threshed, milled and packaged. The milled flour was mixed with water and yeast and baked. Many changes from seed to plant to stalk to threshed seed to flour to bread. The end is a thing of wonder and sustenance.
All: Blessed be!
The bread is handed around.

Accepting Change
Priestess or Participant holding the cider: This is the cider of delight made from the apples of the orchard. Perhaps many years ago, an apple tree was planted. When young, the tree was without branches and was called a maiden tree. Soon it branched and grew. Perhaps 2 or 3 years went by before the tree bloomed, but then it did with a profusion of white 5-petals flowers, which were pollinated by the bees. Once pollinated, the petals fell off the flower and it carefully created a protective home for its seeds. That home, the fruit, grew larger and larger over the summer and changed color. It was picked, crushed and juiced. And now, we have the pleasure of drinking it.
All: Blessed be!
The cider is handed around.

Participant reads:
The Autumn by Elizabeth Barrett Browning (1833)
Go, sit upon the lofty hill,
And turn your eyes around,
Where waving woods and waters wild

Do hymn an autumn sound.
The summer sun is faint on them —
The summer flowers depart —
Sit still — as all transform'd to stone,
Except your musing heart.

How there you sat in summer-time,
May yet be in your mind;
And how you heard the green woods sing
Beneath the freshening wind.
Though the same wind now blows around,
You would its blast recall;
For every breath that stirs the trees,
Doth cause a leaf to fall.

Oh! like that wind, is all the mirth
That flesh and dust impart:
We cannot bear its visitings,
When change is on the heart.
Gay words and jests may make us smile,
When Sorrow is asleep;
But other things must make us smile,
When Sorrow bids us weep!

The dearest hands that clasp our hands, —
Their presence may be o'er;
The dearest voice that meets our ear,
That tone may come no more!
Youth fades; and then, the joys of youth,
Which once refresh'd our mind,
Shall come — as, on those sighing woods,
The chilling autumn wind.
Hear not the wind —
view not the woods;
Look out o'er vale and hill —
In spring, the sky encircled them —

The sky is round them still.
Come autumn's scathe —
Come winter's cold —
Come change —
and human fate!
Whatever prospect Heaven doth bound,
Can ne'er be desolate.

Thanking the Corners

East Participant: We thank the spirits of the East, the spirits of the mind. We thank them for helping us focus on matters of the thought and ideas.
Extinguish the candle of the East.
All: Blessed Be!

South Participant: We thank the spirits of the South, the spirits of the physical body. We thank them for helping us focus on matters of the strength and movement.
Extinguish the candle of the South.
All: Blessed Be!

West Participant: We thank the spirits of the West, the spirits of emotions. We thank them for helping us focus on matters of love and trust.
Extinguish the candle of the West.
All: Blessed Be!

North Participant: We thank the spirits of the North, the spirits of the earth. We thank them for helping us focus on matters of sustenance and endeavor.
Extinguish the candle of the North.
All: Blessed Be!

Priestess: May the spirit of the Goddess, the spirit of oneness with all things, stay with us as we end this ritual.
All: Blessed Be!

Opening the Circle
Ring bell.

All: The Circle is open, but unbroken
May the peace of the Goddess go in our hearts
Merry Meet and Merry Part
And Merry Meet again
Blessed be.

A Ritual of Healing

The Rhythm of Healing

The Rhythm of Healing
Setting up for This Ritual

This ritual could be done at any time of the year, for any holiday — or even a full moon ritual. The Rhythm of Healing ritual was dedicated to several friends who were sick when we developed the ritual.

This is a very simple ritual. All that is needed are enough drums or other percussion instruments for all of the participants. You will also need chairs for everyone, along with a talking stick (a stick often used in Native American celebrations that designates who has the right to speak at a given time), and a poppet to hold the accumulated energy. We used a teddy bear for a poppet, but any doll will do. All that is needed on the altar is the poppet along with a pitcher of water and some glasses, and the directional candles, if they are not at the perimeter of the circle.

The music for Dona Nobis Pacem is available on the web. If you have enough people, sing it as a round.

Some recorded music is needed at the end of the ritual to allow everyone to get calm and mellow -- perhaps some natural sounds or some classical guitar.

The Rhythm of Healing
Order of Ritual

Clearing the Temple
The priestess circles the perimeter of the circle three times with a small drum or rattle.

Priestess: I clear this space for a ritual of spirit and healing. Let all anger, hate, distrust and all other negativity leave this space of power.

Raising the Temple
Priestess: I am going to build the temple. As I do, try to visualize the magic sphere of the temple that we sit within. This is the space we will fill with power. Once it is full, we will send the power out to folks who need the healing, as our part of bringing in the spring.

I raise the temple now. I build a foundation of Gaia's energy. I place a pillar of spring breezes in the East. I place a pillar of fiery power in the South. I place a pillar of flowing blue in the West. I place a pillar of the world tree in the North. Over us, I raise a sparkling roof of the infinite sky. See now the crystal temple of the infinite energy of life that surrounds us.

Calling the Corners
East Participant: I call the power of air for our use in this healing ceremony. Bring us the power to fill the air with healing vibrations.
Light the candle of the East.
All: Blessed be!

South Participant: I call the power of fire for our use in this healing ceremony. Bring us the power to fill the air with healing warmth.
Light the candle of the South.
All: Blessed be!

West Participant: I call the power of water for our use in this healing ceremony. Bring us the power to fill the air with healing emotion.

87

Light the candle of the West.
All: Blessed be!

North Participant: I call the power of earth for our use in this healing ceremony. Bring us the power to fill the air with the strength of Gaia.
Light the candle of the North.
All: Blessed be!

Ring Bell
Priestess: The temple is erected. Let all be here in perfect love and perfect trust. In this time, we stand in the temple that is no place; in a time that is no time.

An Introduction to the Ritual
We called the powers of the elements to help us send healing to those who need it. The east brings us the power of wind, the south brings us the power of the sun, the west brings us the power of the ocean and the north brings us Mother Earth strength and solidity. We can tap into all that energy if we open ourselves to it.

Drumming is a traditional way of gathering energy. The drumming will fill us with the power that the elements hold. If we listen, we can hear the heartbeat of our mother earth in the drumming. We can use this energy for healing those we know and love, as well as those we don't know, but who need our help.

We will each take a turn at leading the drumming, by passing the wand. When you are ready to pass the wand, hold it out and someone who is ready to lead will take it.

Drumming for Healing Energy
Priestess hands wand to lead drummer.
Drumming commences.
Each person takes a turn establishing a rhythm and leading the drumming.

Raising the Power
As the last drummer slows down, the Priestess says: Gather the power from around you and concentrate your energy in your hands. When you are ready, come to the altar and touch the poppet.

Each person, one at a time, gathers her or his energy. When that person feels ready, he or she goes to the poppet and puts a hand on it. When all are at the poppet, we raise the power.

Priestess: Let us raise the power. *We hold hands and together we raise the power.*

Opening the Temple *Once the power is raised, the priestess opens the temple. We raise our arms and send the power out.*

Priestess: I now open the temple. Let the crystal temple become open and porous. Let the energy flow out to all who need it. Let us open the temple of our hearts and let the energy flow out.

All: We send this healing energy out to all who need it.
Priestess: We allow the energy to flow out and the balance to re-establish itself both in the magic circle and in our magic world. *We touch the floor to ground the energy.*

The Sharing of Water
Play recorded music.
Pass glasses of water. Participants drink water.

Ending Song
Sing Dona Nobis Pacem

Thanking the Powers
Participant: We thank the power of the East; the winds bring healing.
Extinguish the candle of the East.
All: Blessed be!

Participant: We thank the power of the South; the sun brings healing.
Extinguish the candle of the South.

All: Blessed be!
Participant: We thank the power of the West; the waters brings healing.
Extinguish the candle of the West.
All: Blessed be!

Participant: We thank the power of the North; the earth's strength brings healing.
Extinguish the candle of the North.
All: Blessed be!

Opening the Circle
Priestess rings bell.

All: The Circle is open, but unbroken
May the peace of the Goddess go in our hearts
Merry Meet and Merry Part
And Merry Meet again
Blessed Be

A Ritual of Personal Empowerment

Crystal Waters

Crystal Waters
Setting up for This Ritual

This is a ritual of cleansing. Originally it was a ritual for Imbolc, but it turns out that it works anytime people want to shed old ideas and become the radiant beings they were meant to be.

I like rituals where participants create something to take home. This is one of those rituals. It does use a lot of items, but it is worth the trouble of collecting them.

Setup
In addition to the usual set of candles, the ritual calls for:
    a broom,
    two pitchers of water,
    a basin to pour the water into,
    a ladle,
    a candle or other fire,
    a bowl of salt,
    a basket or bowl for the crystals,
    small, closeable bottles or jars for each person,
    small crystals, small enough to fit in the bottles.
    Some recorded meditation music, lasting perhaps 3 minutes.

You will also need cider (or wine) with glasses and a nice loaf of bread.

There should be more than enough crystals for everyone, so that the last person to choose a crystal will still have a good selection.

I have not specified songs for this ritual. "I believe I can fly" or Carol King's "Beautiful" or Lennon's "Starting over" would be good, but I am sure you have a song that expresses your feelings about transformation. Remember to send the music out to the participants ahead of time.

Roles for this ritual include the four directions, which I have chosen to call stars in this rite, and a maiden. Optionally, someone other than the priestess could lead the blessing of the crystals.

Crystal Waters
Order of Ritual

We gather at the altar.

Casting the Circle
The Priestess sweeps around the circle three times. She says:
We set this time and place aside for a transformation of energy.
In this place that is no place, and that is all places
In this time that is no time, and that is all time
We stand between the worlds.
The Priestess hands the broom to the Maiden.

Calling the Corners
East Star: Here I bring Light and Air from the East, where the winds
of change rise.
The East Star lights the candle of the East.
All: Blessed Be!

South Star: Here I bring Light and Warmth from the South, where the
sun brings the energy of transformation.
South Star lights the candle.
All: Blessed Be!

West Star: Here I bring Light and Rain from the West, where the
waters swirls in magic patterns.
West Star lights the candle.
All: Blessed Be!

North Star: Here I bring Light and Green Sprouts from the North,
where the trees stand strong.
North Star lights the candle.
All: Blessed Be!

The Maiden rings the bell.

Priestess: The temple is erected, let all who are here, be here in peace and love.

An Introduction to the Ritual

In this ritual, we will first symbolically clean our physical selves by washing our hands, then we will clear our conceptual selves by blessing each part of our beings. We will allow some of the power we gather to pass first into a crystal, and then we will imbue water with some of our collective power. By this action, we will create crystal water that combines our personal, powerful selves with the power of the group. We can each take some of this water home and sprinkle it around the house to clear ghosts of the pasts, bad feelings, sad events and melancholy. Perhaps a drop in the bath could also clear our minds after a confusing day.

The Washing Of Hands

Priestess: We will now wash each other's hands. While we do this, try to envision all the things that impede your life, and visualize those things flowing out of your hands into the basin.

The Priestess puts the basin on the altar and pours water over the maiden's hands and then dries them. The maiden then does the same for the person next to her. The basin, pitcher and towel are passed around the circle clockwise, each person washing the hands of the next. The last person washes the hands of the priestess.

The Priestess goes to the door of the home (first symbolically opening a door in the circle) and tosses the water out the door.
Priestess: Thus, we wash the old thoughts and stale ideas from ourselves. We throw them out with the water.

The Ritual of Self Blessing**

All the participants speak in unison
I bless my feet, that they may walk the path of beauty
I bless my legs, that they may carry me with strength
I bless my hands, that all I do becomes part of the oneness
I bless my genitals, to bring forth my creativity

I bless my solar plexus, that I should stay centered on my path
I bless my heart, that passion and compassion should flow from it
I bless my shoulders, that I carry any burdens with joy
I bless my throat, that I may sing the song of life
I bless my mouth, that I only speak in truth and with kindness
I bless my nose, that the smells of the good earth uplift me
I bless my eyes, that I may see the beauty around me
I bless my third eye, that it may open to truth
I crown myself now with the star of the One.
I stand now in the silver of the Moon and the gold of the Sun.

Song
Sing 'Starting Over" *or* 'I Believe I Can Fly."

Blessing the Crystals
The bottles are passed around the group. Each person takes one.
Maiden pours water from one of the pitchers into basin
Priestess (or participant) blesses the water with salt, sprinkling salt in the water
I purify this water with salt, because the union of water and salt
represent the balance of movement and stability.

Priestess (or participant) blesses the crystals with fire, waving the crystals over the fire.
I bless these crystals with fire, that they remember the fire that
formed them

Priestess (or participant) blesses the crystals with water and salt, sprinkling water over the crystals.
I bless these crystals that they reflect the power of water. I bless them
with salt that they remember the power of the earth they represent.

Priestess (or participant) blesses the crystals with air, waving the crystals over the water.
I bless these crystals with air that they shimmer in the light.
All: Blessed Be!
The crystals are passed around the group. Each person takes one.

The Crystal Meditation

Priestess: Hold the crystal to your solar plexus, feel your connection to the earth. Feel as though you are a tree, feel your roots flow through your legs, through the floor and into the earth. Feel the earth hold you up. Feel yourself balanced on the earth; centered over the center of the earth; part of the structure of the world. Now, feel the earth's strength rising through you, surging through every part of you. You are as strong as the world.

We meditate on the earth's power. Play recorded music if that facilitates meditation.

Priestess: Allow some of that strength and power to flow into the crystal, knowing that, paradoxically, you lose nothing while sharing this power. Look at the crystal and feel it glow. Now, place it in your bottle.

Raising the Power

Priestess: We are all empowered now -- hold hands and share that power. *We hold hands and raise the power over the water.*

Priestess: Now touch the basin of water and watch it take on the power. Ground any leftover energy by touching the floor or the altar.

We hold hands and raise the power over the water.
When the power is raised the priestess says: Now touch the basin of water and watch it take on the power. Ground any leftover energy by touching the floor or the altar.
We each touch the water and then the floor or the altar.

Sharing the Water.

The ladle is handed around and each person fills his or her bottle with the empowered water.
We hold up the bottles.

Participants: Behold the power of transformation. Blessed Be!

Song
Sing "Beautiful" *or* "Starting Over" *or* any other song that fits.

The Simple Feast
Participant: I bless this cider (or wine), the transformation of the harvest.
The cider is poured in glasses and shared.
Participant: I bless this bread, the transformation of the harvest. *The bread is cut and shared.*

Thanking the Corners
The East Star extinguishes the candle of the East. saying:
We thank the spirits of the East for bringing light and air to our ritual. *All:* Blessed Be!

The South Star extinguishes the candle of the South. saying:
We thank the spirits of the South, for bringing light and warmth to our ritual. *All:* Blessed Be!

The West Star extinguishes the candle of the West, saying:
We thank the spirits of the West, for bringing light and crystal water to our ritual. *All:* Blessed Be!

The North Star extinguishes the candle of the North, saying:
We thank the spirits of the North, for bringing strength and beauty to our ritual. *All:* Blessed Be!

Opening the circle
Ring bell.
All: The Circle is open, but unbroken
May the peace of the Goddess go in our hearts
Merry Meet and Merry Part
And Merry Meet again
Blessed Be!

**Adapted from a Navajo Chant, with thanks to them.

Endword

To finish my thoughts: May these rituals are helpful to you in your spiritual journey. Each of us has their individual journey through life. For many of us, ritual is a way of a creating milestones on our way to the future. We grow an appreciation of time as we experience it – the seasons rolling in and out; the wheel of the year turning. And at each turn, we celebrate the change.

Hopefully, this book has given you the experience of working with the things of nature in a spiritual way. I hope it has introduced you to the idea of using symbols to understand a greater reality. These symbols might be physical objects – a potato or an egg – or they might be phenomena like silence or drumming. The potato becomes not a potato, but a stand-in for our fears and indecision which will be transformed by the healing earth. Physical silence quiets our hearts to hear the quiet beauty within.

I am also hoping that this book serves a jumping off platform for you to create your own rituals. Use these as framework to create your own. I know that at least two of my rituals have been scaled up for a large group and one has been adapted for use by children.

Remember that ritual should be fun as well as solemn and everyone has a story of a ritual when something went wrong. It is part of the wonder of being human.

If you want to follow my year of rituals. I blog about them at www.magicinyourlivingroom.com
My blog has photos of our rituals, so you can get a good idea of what we do. Leave me a note about your rituals

May your path be happy and enlightening. Merry Part!

Bright Blessings

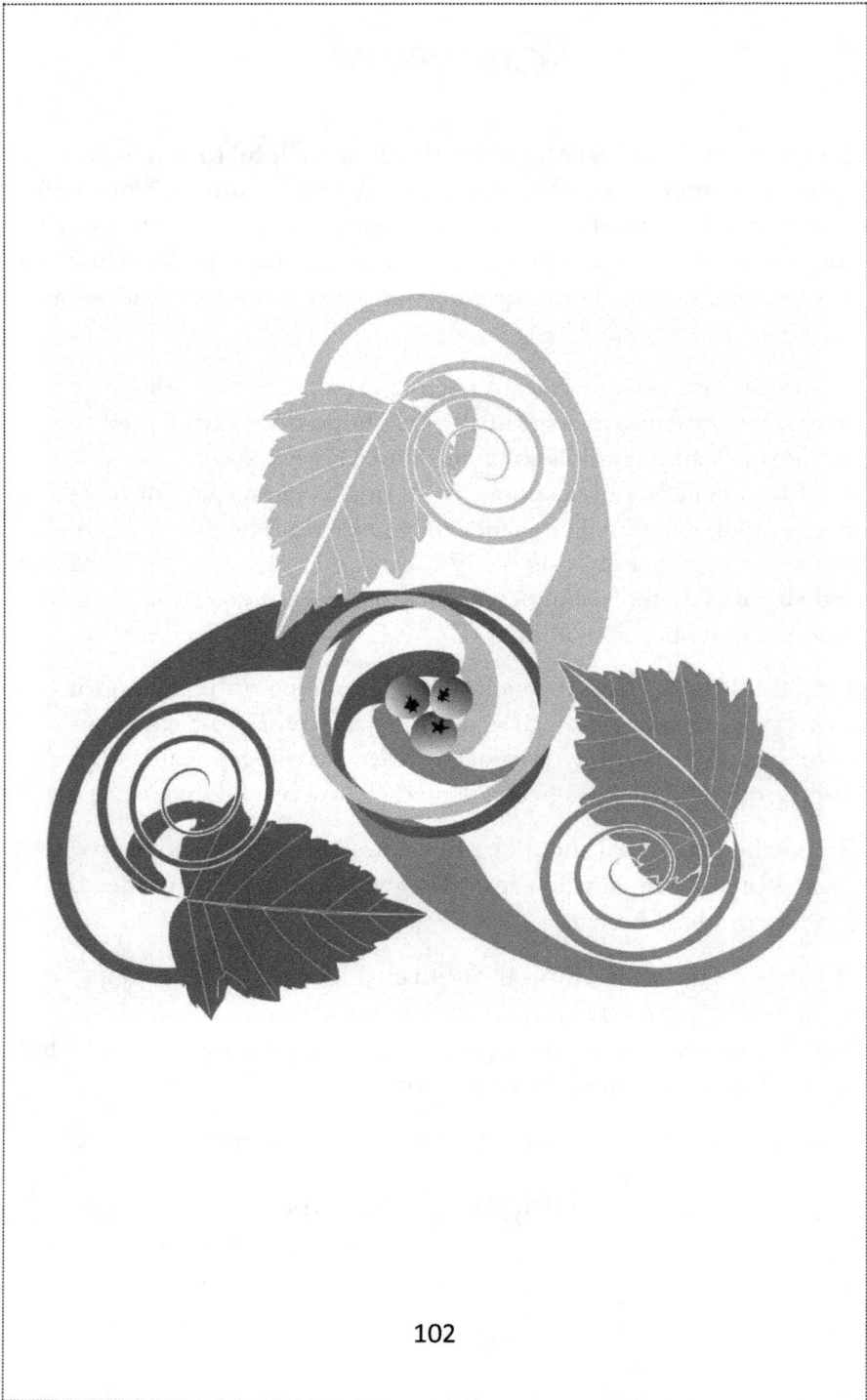

www.ingramcontent.com/pod-product-compliance
Lightning Source LLC
Chambersburg PA
CBHW061151040426
42445CB00013B/1647